# Tomorrow

## Will Be Better

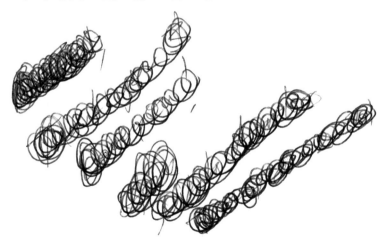

### Nikala Asante

Tomorrow Will Be Better 1

ISBN-13: 978-1508806226

ISBN-10: 1508806225

Tomorrow Will Be Better 2

Dedicated to Martina and Aaliyah.

Shine bright, stars.  Be women who change the world.

# Table of Contents

# Introduction

I first became interested in Human Rights as a small child, although I was unaware of the term *Human Rights*. I had strong values around inclusiveness, fair treatment, justice, and health equity. Here is a story in example:

When my father fell victim to the crack epidemic of the 1980's, my family cut him off to try to get him off drugs. No food, nothing. Despite the fact that he was still married to my mother and they had 3 daughters together, he was not even allowed to visit us openly. He had to sneak to our window to see us. My sisters, perhaps wiser, would ignore his knocking, but I never did.

When I was about 6 years old, living with my grandmother, I started stealing food for my father. Whenever he knocked on my bedroom window, I would pack up whatever food was leftover in the kitchen and leave with him, not understanding that this was theft and kidnapping. All I knew was that we were family, and family meant everybody was included. To me, family meant unconditional love.

However, as much as I wanted him to be included, I did not want it to be at the price of harm of other family members. When my father visited us to yell at or physically abuse my mother, I would run after him screaming in her defense. Like David of the Bible, I was somehow confident that my little body could overcome his large one. This boldness was uncalculated. It was based on an early spirit for justice. Maybe you have done something similar because of your love for justice.

In the realm of health, if anyone was sick, I would lay my little hands on them and pray. My grandmother told me that my prayers always made her ailments go away, so I embraced my position as a youth prayer warrior very seriously. Both of my brothers had serious health issues that I thought I could heal with my hands too. Chuckie had sickle cell anemia and Jeff had a heart defect. By the time that I was 10, I lost both of them. Chuckie was 16 and Jeff was 21. I wondered how that could have happened when I had prayed for them. That's when I came to understand that prayer had its limitations.

While prayer can be effective to an extent, I have now learned about healthy foods, herbs, and avoidance of dangerous chemicals that perhaps could have saved my grandmother and my brothers. I also share what I have learned about health with people in other countries to help them too. And then at times, nothing works. That's okay too. If it is time for one to go, we can still honor their spirit after physical death.

--

As I shared, I was raised by my grandmother, a true Wonder Woman. Her house was like a hostel, usually lodging fourteen to twenty family members at a time, including my mother and my two sisters. Uncles, aunts, cousins, and friends also took positions in beds or on the floor. She took care of most of our shelter and food with money that she brought in from running a night club and a farm. Everyone else offered some contribution of importance based on what they could give from where their life was during that time. When my grandmother passed away, our basic needs became insecure. This was the point where for a while, my life seemed to fall from under me.

My father returned to our household after my grandmother's death, now rehabilitated, and took a regular job. He recognized that his minimum wage job was not enough to provide for a wife and three children, so he began selling crack, a common way to make money where we lived. This choice led to him serving four years in prison. This was his second or third long stint of incarceration during my childhood years.

The instability of our household coupled with my mother struggling to preserve her own sanity resulted in a space in my life where I felt like I was on a killing field. From age 14 to 18, unprotected by my father, brothers, and uncles, all of which were in jail or deceased at this point, I was subjected to robberies, physical and sexual assaults, and other traumatic experiences.

At the age of 17, I moved in with my boyfriend, perhaps looking for protection and stability. After 8 months of cohabitating, he hit me for the first time. I packed my bags and left immediately. I went back to the apartment that I shared with my sister and her best friend, but within days I found out that I was pregnant. After talking with my family and with my boyfriend, we felt the "Christian"* thing to do was to stay together since we were having a child together.

The physical abuse did not happen all the time – maybe once every 6 or 9 months. More often, we had arguments about petty things or his jealousy. It

---

* I no longer feel that this is representative of Christianity. If someone hits you, leave. Period.

seemed like we argued every day. We had our good moments too – he was the most attentive and affectionate man that I have ever been in a relationship with. He would buy me flowers, cards, or teddy bears after fights. Then, he would cry about how his mother left him, his father died, and his past girlfriends took advantage of his kindness. I had been through a lot of pain too, so I wanted to be there for him no matter what. I wanted to demonstrate a love and loyalty greater than any I had ever experienced. In hindsight, this was not the best choice.

During this time, I was working two waitressing jobs. I dropped out of high school in 11th grade because I would fall asleep in school after working 12 -16 hours a day – from the time that I got out of school until early the next morning with only a quick cat nap before classes. Even with working all of these hours, it was not uncommon to finish a 16 hour day with around $50 after paying for food. Life was very hard.

My son's father worked too, but we were not advancing financially. He controlled our money and sometimes chose to use large portions frivolously on drugs, alcohol, or electronics. My days were often long and stressful. Despite my sacrifices, I saw no advancement, and my home felt like a prison. If you had asked me that year what I saw for my future, I really wouldn't have been able to answer. I was focused on day-to-day survival.

It's funny how being in the wrong relationship can have your life caught up like that. We often repeat the types of relationships that we see in our families. As a child, no matter how my father disappointed me or hurt my mother, I would forgive him. I didn't understand how this could form into an unhealthy pattern of accepting dysfunction. As I write this, I am 29 years old and have set a standard for myself to never accept abuse or dysfunction from any relationship. This choice has helped me to live a beautiful, free and purpose filled life. I hope that in reading this book, you can learn from my mistakes and from my successes to live a life even greater than mine.

## Let's Dialogue!

What are the 5 things that you are most passionate about in life?

Have you ever been in an unhealthy relationship with a boyfriend or girlfriend? If so, what was it like?

What kind of relationship do your parents have with each other? If you really think about it, how would you say this affects your relationships?

Imagine that it is 10 years from today. Write down 10 of the things that you will be doing this year, 10 years in the future. Have fun with it! (i.e.: making $80,000, chilling with my spouse in

Italy for vacation, holding a food drive at my church, skydiving... whatever!)

_____

_____

_____

_____

_____

_____

_____

_____

_____

--

As you make your life and relationship decisions, keep this ideal life in mind. If your choices are taking you away from the type of life that you want, then it is time to re-evaluate your choices.

As I am sitting here writing to you, my little sister is sitting in prison, maybe writing to me. We write to each other often.  We have the same dad and different moms.  Her mom passed away when she was 14 due to health problems, and our dad did not do a good job taking over.  At the time, he was off drugs, but he was still battling alcoholism.  It got so bad living with him that she moved out on her own at 16.

Shortly after, she got caught up with an older man, who maybe presented a father figure.  She was 16 and he was 32.  The rap songs call the 'hood the "trap" for a reason.  There are so many ways that life can come down on you, like metal claws on a struggling animal.  This boyfriend of hers decided that he wanted to come up quickly, so he plotted a robbery.  She rode with him to show her loyalty.  What she didn't know is that he was planning to kill the victim.

She is now 21 and has been in prison for the past 5 years.  She was sentenced to 15 years total, the best years of her life.  I cannot cry enough tears for her. She is so brilliant and so talented, but made a terrible decision. Again, plan out your goals and if anyone suggests anything that may possibly take you away from that, run from that person like your life depends on it. It does.

--

## Sestet to a Sister in Silence

Accusing, he tore through her diary pages
Seeking secrets that did not exist
Perfection, aggressively interrupted
By a "bitch!", a palm, a fist, and
Shattered, into what now is mosaic
Beautiful, if held at a distance.

## Lil' Tre[†]

They got the white cars,
They got the blue lights,
We pace the streets,
We feel out of place;

---

[†] Based on "Old Lem" by Sterling A. Brown.

They sweep the block,
They settle the fights,
We best be thankful
For being "safe";

3am, gunshots outside,
Block out the voices,
Block out the screams;

We got to say "Mistuh,
Here's my ID,
No, I was not outside at 3,
No, no one was in the house, but me,
No, you cannot come in and see."

They got the nightsticks,
They got the Tasers,
We hold our heads down,
Pray they won't take us,
They got the judges,

We got the cases,
They got the lawyers,
Who fail to save us;

I had a friend
With nothing to see,
But cousins in jail,
Shoot-outs on TV,
By age of 10,
He was rollin' up trees,
By age of 13,
He was hittin' the scene;

Shotguns and .45s,
Eyes-on-spinners-and-chains,
Screwdrivers and hot-wires,
Hennessy-and-cocaine;

By age of 18,
That boy was a lifer,

Ten more in the graveyard,
With a life just like him;
If the system served us,
It would look at the basis,
Educate, rehabilitate,
Not lock 'em in cages;

They got the white cars,
We still got power,
We stop killing each other,
We educate ours,
We take pride in our hoods,
We build and we grow,
We study, we learn,
We share what we know.

# Chapter 1: You Ain't Stupid, Though

I recently talked to a 14 year old who did not know 72 divided by 9. Let's call him Devon. Devon attends a school where they don't even let him bring the textbooks home to study. Furthermore, the standardized testing is a joke. They just keep passing him to the next grade anyway. Do you know someone like this? This is the type of ish that will have you mad at the world. You see kids yelling at their parents or teachers, "I'm not stupid!" because they really do feel stupid. But you know what? They're really not. Even Devon. He *can* learn, but a lot of his teachers are probably not even trying because (even though they won't say it), they think he's stupid too.

Have you ever walked towards a squirrel outside and it ran up a tree? Why does it do that? It's afraid, right? It has a good reason to be afraid. Maybe, some of his cousins have been trapped or shot by hunters. He has a reason to be defensive. It's the same situation with Devon -- he feels stupid for good reason. The trick to empowerment for Devon, or for you, or for anyone else, is to pinpoint the origin of the negative self-image. This is a part of being solution-oriented. Devon feeling stupid is a *problem.* This problem must be *solved.* Glazing it over by telling him, "You ain't stupid," does not solve the problem.

Yes, Devon, you feel stupid. You feel stupid because you have been the victim of a system instituted to *deliberately* deprive you of the knowledge that you need to thrive in this world. This was done through attacks and distractions. You have been attacked through your food - chemicals, pesticides, hormones, genetic modifications, addictive substances, fragrances, and colorants - all of which were intended to enslave your mind and body to corporations.

What can you do about it? You can cut down fast food, meat, and processed food (boxed and packaged foods). You can make it a point to eat fresh fruits and vegetables daily, organic when you can get it. You can research the ingredients of products that you use like shampoo and soap, and try to get the ones with less or no dangerous chemicals. When you put something on your skin, it goes into your body and affects you just like if you ate it.

You have been attacked through the media. You saw Black men in dresses and fat-suits, as drug dealers and crooks, as the whores and pimps. Jokes - hardly ever as the geniuses and main characters. More often, they were sidekicks or those needing to be saved by a benevolent White person. Even Django needed a White savior. *Blood Diamond. The Blind Side.* And on the music videos, you saw your favorite rappers pouring good liquor on "bad b*tches". Isn't it strange that it is usually not Black men who own these music companies and decide how these videos are going to look?

Who decided that every hit song repeated on the radio would tell you to sell drugs, have lots of sex, get drunk, or shoot somebody? Who decided to tell your sisters to drop it low, bounce it, and bust it open on every other song? Hell, we know the words "drop it low" before we can count to ten – it seems like someone is trying to keep us low, for real.

You were attacked through your education. You were taught about "great" European "heroes" such as Christopher Columbus and George Washington – the man who started the freakin' Transatlantic Slave Trade and a slave owner. Both were the enemies of your ancestors. But, you were instructed to "remember the Alamo" and forget slavery. Martin Luther King Jr. was presented to persuade you to "turn the other cheek" to atrocities, while the bulk of his ideology was never introduced to you. Malcolm X, if teachers taught about him at all, was presented as an "advocate of violence" or the opposite of Dr. King. You never learned how peaceful that he really was[‡].

---

[‡] Read *Malcolm X: By Any Means Necessary* by Walter Dean Myers.

Devon, your education denied you true advancement because it made your culture seem minimal. Did you ever learn about any African history before we were enslaved in the United States? Did your textbooks tell you anything about our great civilizations in ancient Africa§? Did you learn that a Black man was the first known doctor, Imhotep, or that Black men invented things that we use every day now like the first pen and the first calendar? And why is it that out of the millions of African-Americans that have lived and died on American soil, there are only 10 or so that are taught in your textbooks each year, and usually in February? The shortest month. You have been lied to.

You have been attacked. And now, it is time for us to heal. But to prevent further damage, we need armor. That armor is knowledge, because knowledge really is power. What you don't know can

---

§ Read *Lessons from History: Advanced Edition* by Jawanza Kunjufu.

kill you, mentally or physically. Are you ready to choose life?

--

### System Failure

How we living?
Imhotep built the first pyramid,
Rayshawn built matchstick clocks in prison,
Nzinga brought her people together,
Lisa brought her children to a domestic
violence shelter,
Now, who can say that's not activism?

Madame CJ Walker made millions,
Grandma Mable raised children,
While baking pies for the church, doing farm
work, and
Organizing the whole family for Christmas and
Thanksgiving.

Tyrone is on the grind from 9 to 9,

Investing time in a business
That will get him time,
He has a mathematical mind
Like Benjamin Banneker who planned
Washington DC,
But for Tyrone,
The trap is all that he sees.

And Reesie, wants to reach for the stars
Like Jemison, Mae,
She's in high school,
But her reading level is Third Grade,
She rep blue, like her cousin
Who was shot by a gang, bang!
Barack made it, but he wasn't
From her hood
So it ain't the same thang --

System.  Failure.
System.  Failure.

We have all the historic traits
Of the greats
But the current paradigm
Doesn't allow for operate-
Tion, at a level beyond
Mininum Wage, Amalgamation, or the
Gun.

System.  Failure.
System.  Failure.
Reboot, reconstitute
How who you are
Translates into what you do
So the new standard of operation
Can be you.

# Let's Dialogue!

Have you ever felt stupid?  If so, was there a particular situation that made you feel this way?

Take it Home!

1. Go to your kitchen and pick out a boxed or packaged item that you ate this week.  Snap a picture of the ingredients and look each one up online in this format:

   Dangers of:

   _____

   Health Benefits of:

   _____

   You will find that some ingredients have both dangers and benefits.  Those are ingredients that you want to cut down, but maybe not cut out. Some ingredients, however, will have only dangers and no benefits. Those are ingredients that you want to cut out.

--

## The Music Test

Does music contribute to mind control? If so, what is it controlling our minds to think? Let's investigate!

Do an internet search of the top five Billboard Rap songs. Now, pull up the lyrics of each of these 5 songs. Copy them to a Word document or print them out. Then, answer these questions about each song:

> a. How many times does the song mention or suggest sex?

b. How many times does the song mention or suggest drugs?

c. How many times does the song mention or suggest alcohol or getting drunk?

d. How many times does the song mention or suggest violence?

e. How many times does the song use the words b*tch, n*gga, or hoe?

f. Does the song promote being capitalism centered (a lot of emphasis on money)? Underline each line that refers to this concept.

g. Does the song promote being individualistic (f*ck them other n*ggas or b*tches, I'm all I got, I got enemies, etc...)? Underline each line that refers to this concept.

Now, read the following passage by Dr. John Schinnerer.**

> "Favorite songs are listened to over and over hundreds or thousands of times so it makes good sense to speculate that music lyrics may have a profound impact on the listener's perception of the world, other people, and which emotions are experienced as well as the frequency of those emotions... Priming is when a person is exposed to certain stimulus, such as words, lyrics, or surroundings, and their subconscious mind is activated. Once activated, the person tends to act in ways that are consistent with the stimulus without awareness of why they are behaving in that manner."

What are your thoughts about the passage above? If it is true, how would the lyrics that

---

** http://drjohnblog.guidetoself.com/2009/06/29/how-do-song-lyrics-affect-your-brain-lyrics-prime-the-brain-for-good-and-bad/

you read affect the listeners when they are heard over and over?

--

Don't get me wrong, I *love* rap music. I listen to Hip Hop more than I listen to any other genre of music. But maybe, it's time for us to start writing our own lyrics and producing our own songs that promote the kind of behavior that we want to see in the world. Sometimes, we don't want to listen to music that's too positive because the aim is to "teach" us, and who wants to hear teaching and preaching all the time? At the same time, everything is teaching us *something*. We just have to be aware of what we are being taught.

# List of Songs to Check Out††

- WuTang Clan – C.R.E.A.M.
- Lupe Fiasco – I'm Beamin'
- Black Star – Thieves in the Night
- Sa-Roc feat. David Banner – The Who?
- Kool Moe Dee – I Go To Work
- Nas – I Know I Can
- J. Cole – Love Yours
- Tupac – Keep Ya Head Up
- Grandmaster Flash and the Furious Five – The Message
- The ReMINDers – You Can Count on Me
- Immortal Technique – You Never Know
- Outkast – Liberation
- David Sha feat. Riders Against the Storm – Broken Record
- SWAT - African Drum
- Lauryn Hill – Lost Ones Z-Ro – These Days
- Janelle Monae – Q.U.E.E.N.
- Pete Rock and CL Smooth – Take You There
- Public Enemy – Fight the Power
- Kendrick Lamar – Hiii Power; His Pain
- D Arthur – Break Away
- K Rino – Problems
- Dead Prez – Malcolm Garvey Huey
- Dee 1 – Against Us
- DeMarcus Rashad – Conscious Sounds

---

†† Some songs have mature language.

# Chapter 2: How Suicide Saved My Life

This is the story that I don't tell. This is the unheroic story. This is the part that always gets left out. People often ask me what the turning point was in my life. They ask when I decided that I was really going to pursue the path that I am on now. I respond that I wanted to be a good role model and make a good life for my son and I, but this is only part of the story.

When I decided to take my life down this path, it was after my third suicide attempt. My first suicide attempt was when I was 16. I had been a victim of molestation and multiple rapes at this point, my father was in prison, and my mother was disconnected. Every time that I tried to get close to her during this period, she would push me away; perhaps, because of the pain that she was experiencing in her own life.

I was drinking alcohol every day, smoking marijuana, and popping ecstasy. I was still in school and waiting tables – but not truly engaged in either. I did not have any future plans. I was struggling to find worth in my life and was not finding it. So one night, I took most of a bottle of Midol and drank most of a bottle of Thunderbird with it, a really strong cheap alcohol.

I got sick that night and had to go to the hospital, but I did not die. I felt that maybe I just did not know how to do it right. So, I continued my routine of work and school. However, I was still depressed.

My second suicide attempt was when I was 19 years old. I felt like my life was at an impassable brick wall. My son's father regularly verbally and physically attacked me over false assumptions that I was cheating or that I would leave. I was not able to get assistance from the police or from my family that would protect me.

Everyone either said that I should stay with him because we had a child together or that I would "go back anyway" if they helped me leave, without ever giving me an opportunity to prove that I wanted to be away from him. I felt that there was nowhere to go.

As I was preparing to take my GED test one morning, he began punching and kicking me the worst ever – something about taking too long washing clothes. I'm sure it was because he had a fear that education would separate us. When I tried to fight back, he choked me until I nearly passed out and then pushed me into a closet and beat me with wire hangers and shoes. I kept fighting back, but he was stronger.

My face was mangled and I was just thinking that my mother would think that I was a failure for not going to take the GED test that day. He wouldn't let me use the phone or leave the house, because people would know what he had done. I screamed, but my neighbors never called the police. So, as soon as I could gather strength to get to the bathroom, I swallowed what was left of a bottle of Tylenol, hoping that it was stronger than the Midol. It was maybe 20 to 30 pills. I stood in front of the mirror, catching my breath, feeling that I had won. I could die and he could not control it like he controlled the rest of my life.

When I re-entered the bedroom, I laid down still bloody and told him that nothing mattered anymore because I'd be dead soon. When he realized what I had done, he blocked the bedroom door with furniture and stood over me, cursing and screaming, "You're going to Hell." He taunted me, saying things like, "Oh, if you think I'm going to let you go to the hospital, you're wrong, bitch. You're going to die."

I lay there throwing up bile on the side of the bed until my insides felt completely dry. But I didn't die. Though I didn't leave that day, that episode was the end of the relationship for me. I knew that I had to find a way to leave. My son's father was arrested for violating probation shortly thereafter. I knew that he would not be in jail for long, so I arranged to move in with a friend in Atlanta for a few weeks while I found a job and an apartment for me and my son. My son and I remained in Atlanta for almost 2 years.

Things were going pretty well for about the first year and a half, but just before winter, I lost my job. Our gas was turned off and my family and friends were unable to help. I started doing freelance graphic design and promotions work, but it was not panning out to enough money. We were so cold, with no heat and no hot water. Most of our meals were variations of Ramen noodles.

I started having severe debilitating migraine headaches. I went to the doctor and they said that I may a have cancerous tumor and to come back for an MRI. I was feeling like it couldn't possibly get any worse, until I came home from the doctor that day. My neighbor had an apartment fire that hit a gas line.

My whole apartment building exploded. My son and I lost everything and had to start over once again.

I felt like such a loser. I felt that nothing that I attempted would ever be successful. My mother was pretty stable by then and offered to pay for our flight to come and live with her in Texas. My son's father had moved to another state by this time and gotten married to another woman. I was still depressed. I had no diploma, no GED, no driver's license even. I was 22 years old.

My plan was to return to Texas, write a book about my life, and then commit suicide. I was exhausted from the failures of my life and just wanted it to end. I felt that I could do it right this time. Also, I wanted my son to be with family when I did it, so that he would not be put in foster care. When I arrived at my mother's house, I sat and typed and typed – over 90 pages – until I felt that my life was really represented. Then, I slept.

The next day, I woke up and reread what I wrote. I wanted to make sure that my life was accurately depicted before I ended it. As I read over it, I realized that my life was all about what had happened to me, and not at all about what I had made happen. My story was one of tragedy after tragedy with no triumph. I had done nothing of substance. I had left no legacy for my son or future descendants. I have heard that is a moment that many older people have on their deathbeds – looking back on their lives and realized that they never *lived.* Thankfully, I was still young. You see, shit can be used for fertilizer to grow a beautiful garden. It can be powerful. But if you don't use that shit to grow anything, it's just shit. I began making plans to use my skills and talents to their fullest potential. I would never attempt suicide again. I would live fully and authentically and leave great big giant footsteps for my son to follow, or die trying.

This is not a story that I tell, because suicide is a taboo in the Black community, and because it's just such a sensitive topic for me. If you are also dealing with feelings of worthlessness, seek help.

When I went to Haiti in May 2014, I asked a room of nursing students how they coped after witnessing thousands of deaths, including losses of family members during the 2010 earthquake. I asked them if they had ever felt suicidal during the roughest times. They said no, never, because even if today was bad, tomorrow would be better. Tomorrow always has the potential to be better.

## Let's Dialogue!

Have you or a friend ever felt suicidal? If so, what helped to get past that point and start enjoying life again?

One reason that people become depressed is because they feel that they have no viable skills or talents. Think of 5 things that you are really good at. If you have trouble thinking of 5 things, make a commitment to become really good at least one new thing this year.

Make a list here of 10 things that you like about yourself:

_____

_____

_____

_____

_____

_____

_____

_____

_____

_____

# Chapter 3: Trekking the Triangle

We have all learned about the Trans-Atlantic Triangle in school – the triangular route along which the slave trade occurred. Some more fittingly call it the *African Holocaust,* because during this time, millions of African people were robbed of their freedom or killed in the struggle against enslavement.

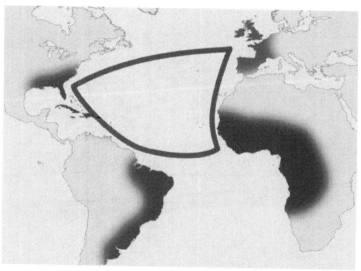

The path of the African Holocaust‡‡ trailed from

the United States, where settlers from Europe sailed to Africa to kidnap or purchase human beings, to the Caribbean, where millions of African people were enslaved, back to the United States, where millions of African people were also enslaved. The fourth point of this path is the original home of the enslavers and colonizers – Europe. Europeans began the Trans-Atlantic Slave Trade even before they began settling in the United States.

I have been fortunate to travel to Europe, Africa, the Caribbean, and of course within my home country, the United States. The purpose of each one of my journeys has been grounded in a desire to contribute to the advancement of people of the African Diaspora. I would like to share some observations and experiences from my travels. But first, I would like to briefly discuss a little history for context.

## What is an African Diaspora anyway?

*The African Diaspora* consists of African people around the world who have been spread by voluntary or forced migration[§§]. In other words, *Black people around the world* form the African Diaspora. Large concentrations of Black migrants outside of Africa are in the Caribbean and in the United States, mainly because of the African Holocaust, but you can find Black people literally all over the world. Whether you are in Canada, Europe, Australia, India, China, or anywhere else, you will find Black people. There was even a Black Arctic explorer, Matthew Henson.

MATTHEW A. HENSON IMMEDIATELY AFTER THE SLEDGE
JOURNEY TO THE POLE AND BACK

---

[§§] Definition from *Introduction to Black Studies* by Dr. Maulana Karenga.

# How Did the Slave Trade Begin?

Just about everyone in America learned about Christopher Columbus in school. I remember in maybe the first grade at my school we sang, "Christopher Columbus sailed the ocean blue in 1492." I was misinformed by my teachers that Columbus discovered the United States, that he ate a peaceful Thanksgiving dinner with Native Americans, and that he proved that the world was not flat, but round. None of this was true.

By the time that I was in high school, I independently learned that European settlers such as Columbus slaughtered many Native Americans to take their land and resources. Then, by my early twenties, I learned Columbus never set foot in the United States and that he was actually the father of the African Holocaust. In other words, he was the person who started the enslaving of Black people in America.

## Hispaniola and the Birth of the Slave Trade

Christopher Columbus first landed on the island now known as Hispaniola. This is an island in Central America shared by two countries, Dominican Republic and Haiti. He and his men attempted to enslave the people who already lived on the island – the Tainos. The Tainos' bodies not respond well to the extremely hard work and the European diseases, so most of them died quickly. Christopher Columbus and his men then had the idea to use Africans from West Africa to work the land instead.

The colonizers thought that West Africans would be strong enough to do the work, but would not know the land well enough to revolt effectively. Also, they would be too far from home to run away. Contrary to this projection, West Africans did revolt regularly. They even jumped off the slave ships into the Atlantic Ocean to avoid being in captivity. The European response to this was to commit tortures so atrocious that no one would want to attempt escape for fear of excruciating pain or for fear of endangering their friends and family.

I don't want to gross you out too much by describing the types of tortures. Some involved burying Africans to be eaten alive by ants or lighting gunpowder inside their bodily orifices. There is a book titled *The Black Jacobins* by C.L.R. James that details further if you are interested. What I will share with you is that the work was so hard, and the tortures were so monstrous, that by the time an enslaved African reached the island of Hispaniola, they would only live 3 more years, on average. That many people were dying!

As I mentioned earlier, Hispaniola was divided into two countries which are now called Haiti and Dominican Republic. To elaborate a little more on how it came to be that these two very different countries are on one island, Haiti was colonized by the French and the Dominican Republic was colonized by the Spanish (from Spain). In other words, most of Haiti's land, resources, and people were owned by the French. It was the same for Dominican Republic and Spain.

How did the Europeans pull this off? Well, mainly with guns. When one group of people has more advanced technology than another group of people, the first can gain power over the latter. That's why it is so important for you to study science and technology. Otherwise, someone may one day have power over you.

## Haiti: The Revolution

From here forward, we will refer to the enslaved Africans brought to *Ayiti* (the original name of Haiti) as Haitians. So, the work that the Haitians were doing was mainly outdoors, because we had not entered the more industrialized age. Many worked in fields picking sugarcane, which like picking cotton, cuts your hands. It is kind of ironic, because when we think of sugar and cotton, we think of sweetness and softness. Once they are processed, we do gain a lot of pleasure from these products. But in their raw forms, they cause a lot of pain. Sugarcane leaves tiny slits on the hands like paper cuts. The sweet fluid around the cuts attracted fire ants, so that the Haitians' hands and arms were constantly inflamed with cuts and bites. In captivity, the Haitians also grew tobacco, raw plants for indigo dye, and many other cash crops.

As you can imagine, this is the type of work that pisses you off every day. It doesn't matter if you have been there for your whole life, you're plotting on how to make it end; not just for you, but for your future generations. The Haitians got fed up. They planned a revolution.

One night, when everything was quiet on the plantations, a man named Boukman led a ceremony that quietly celebrated the initiation of a battle that would change Haiti forever. Thousands of the enslaved exited their beds on a secret cue and burned down over 900 plantations, many killing their masters. Some were loyal and helped their masters escape, but still joined the riots to make sure that their people would be free once and for all.

As you can imagine, the French were pissed off. As mad as they were, they had a big war going on in France that took up all their money and soldiers, The French Revolution. Maybe you learned about it in school. They didn't have the resources to overcome the newly formed Haitian army. Also, over the years that the French had brought in more and more West Africans, and these Africans had more and more babies, the Haitians had come to outnumber the French masters that oversaw them on the island. But now that the Haitians were free, they had a new problem to overcome – rebuilding the country with their own leadership.

Four men were very important to this time – Toussaint L'ouverture, Jean-Jacques Toussaint, Alexandre Petion, and Henri Christophe. In short, these were the men who led the army and rebuilt the country. Have you ever read anything about Napoleon? A short really mean French general? Well, this was during the time that he became emperor of France. Once The French Revolution was over, Napoleon sent his men to re-enslave Haiti. The Haitians beat those men bloody. They were not giving up their freedom. So, the French tried a new trick. They placed an embargo on Haiti so that Haiti could not trade with other countries. This meant that Haiti could not advance financially and eventually become a "developed" country like the United States or countries in Europe.

Before gaining its freedom, Haiti had been the number one exporter in the Caribbean. Imagine if you were working at a company and you were the number one salesperson – making the company millions of dollars every year. But, the company took all of your money and left you with nothing. You would quit that job so you could make the millions for yourself, right? But now imagine that everyone who you could possibly sell your goods to, the company blocked you from reaching.  They were even willing to use violence to keep you away, and recruited all their homies to use violence against you too.  Then, they told you that the only way that you could sell to anyone is if you paid them $800,000 a year out of each million you make, even though you don't even work for them anymore!

That's pretty much what happened to Haiti. France ordered them to pay reparations for freeing themselves from slavery.  In other words, they had to pay France every year to have the potential to even make a little money.  Crazy, I know, right?  On top of that, France and other countries would park warships off Haiti's coast and bully the Haitians for money regularly, like greedy fat kids punking some new kid on the block.  When Haiti didn't have enough money to pay, France had them to cut down trees or give other natural resources.  This is one of the major causes of Haiti being such a poor country now.  When you see pictures of all those starving kids and poor people, you now know some of the history behind it.

# Chapter 4: Tomorrow Will Be Better - Lessons Learned in Haiti

Though Haiti was the last country that I have visited, it is the first country on this side of the Atlantic to be affected by the Trans-Atlantic Slave Trade. So, that is where I will begin telling you about my travel experiences. As of today, I have been to Haiti four times. By the time that you read this, I will probably have traveled there many more times, as I plan to go at least three times a year to do projects that can help people get clean water, fresh food, preventative health care, and good education.

My first trip to Haiti was in August 2013. With a small group of fellow students, I walked in from the Dominican Republic, where we had been interviewing garment workers to help them get better pay and safety conditions in their factories. We accomplished this by coming back to the United States and talking with the buyers about what was really going on. As we crossed the border into Haiti, what stood out to me most was a deaf mute boy being beat by Dominican border guards for a reason that was unclear. The boy was crying out in sounds, not words, and did not appear to understand what was happening. The guards had rifles and AK-47s while the boy did not even have on a decent shirt and pants.

The Dominican Republic and Haiti have a tense and complicated history with each other. Our first day crossing into Haiti, we wanted to observe what was happening at the Border Market so that we could report it from the perspective of seeing it with our own eyes. This makeshift mall was basically just a big concrete warehouse where the Dominicans let the Haitians come sell stuff that they had gathered from charity drops. Imagine, big trucks rolling into Haiti every day with a bunch of stuff that Americans have donated to help the needy. Some of these items are helpful, like food. Some are not helpful, like blenders, when most have no electricity to power them.

Haitians run and collect all of this stuff – some to keep and some to sell. They need the money to eat, to get to work if they have a job, and to send their children to school. School is not free in Haiti.

Before the border market opens at 8:00 am, thousands of Haitians are lined up behind a barbed wire fence waiting to get in and find a good spot to set up what they have collected to sell. Our group got there around 7:00 am and stood near the gate. A border guard instructed us to move back because the Haitians were "like animals" that will "stampede you over". What an insensitive thing to say about human beings trying to live and feed their children!

Near us, there was a shallow river that ran parallel to the border. The border actually bridged over it. This river was famous for being the site where over 40,000 Haitian men, women, and children were murdered with machetes in 1937 so that the Dominicans could push Haiti's border back and make their own country larger. Dominicans are not bad people. There was just a horrible president in office at that time and his name was Rafael Trujillo. He was like Hitler and the Devil put together.

When Trujillo decided to undertake this tragic initiative, no one could tell the difference between a Haitian and a Dominican really, because they were both Black. So, the test to see if a Black person was Haitian or Dominican was to ask them to say the word *perejil,* which is parsley in Spanish. If they didn't roll the r like a Dominican, off with their head.

I write all of this to set up the context for a poem that I wrote while there, which may better illustrate my experience. We were frightened young Americans, scared of the military police, the experience, and the possible dangers. As we watched Haitians press through the opening gate running towards economic opportunity, we pushed ourselves back against the wall of the immigration building bracing ourselves against each other.

While they may have hoped to make five or ten dollars so that they wouldn't have to starve or sell their bodies, we held expensive phones and cameras, afraid to be touched by the very people that we were there to help – so many contradictions. These are the realities and contradictions that you too may experience if you begin to take these journeys. Can you imagine?

### Dajabon Border Market

We stand en masse
Near the Massacre River
Sneaking pictures with i-phones
Cringing from native touch


A thousand bodies
Poised behind barbed wire
Where blood spilled like hibiscus
For parsley's "r"


What did the border guard say to the gringos?

"These Haitians are like animals,
They'll stampede you over."
Queue the laugh track.


Reflect:
Like Columbus and his *compañeros*
stampeded the heart of Hispaniola?
Like Walmart and Chiquita building their
empires on neo-plantations?


Reflect:
For every heaven, there is a hell,
I wipe the sweat from my cheekbones.
To my left, a graceful girl with bantu twists
speeds ahead
A warrior queen
In the throb of pulsing bodies
In a prom dress and flip flops
Charity clothing
She sold her Tom's shoes for mangoes,

Plantains,

Black beans.

On her head,

A cooler.

She'll vend dried fish and peanuts,

A mall up in minutes

At the hands of the poor.


And then,

A boy, maybe 15

Gatorade, on his shoulders

Three 4 by 6 cases

An Atlas under the world.


And then,

A young woman

Holding only a baby,

What did she come for?

What will she sell?

Reflect:

Last night, you grabbed everything valuable

Rice, garlic - left by the UN,

Your daughter's shoes,

Your grandmother's purse,

Sell it, sell it,

Your hope, your soul, your dignity,

Sell it,

Keep only survival.


Your shanty,

Built with wood from a charity drop box

Plastic scraps for roofing

Cardboard for a door.


Reflect:

You don't cry, you collect,

Straw hats for tourists,

Cough syrup,

Noodles,

Bubble gum,

Ceramic vases,

Tennis balls (did they think you would play

tennis?),

From descendants of the men who raped your

country

You collect, anything you can sell.

8:15am

You are at the border market

Your feet aching

From waiting at the gate since 2:00.


Your bag unfurls,

A flag of red beneath you,

You clutch your rosary,

And imagine a God that looks like your

oppressor,

You pray and you wait,

You pray and you wait.


--

After leaving the border market, we slept in Dominican Republic. Let me tell you about something crazy that happened that night in the DR. We went to a local restaurant to get fried chicken, beans, rice, and salad. Many of the students were vegetarian, like me, and did not eat the chicken.

None of our Dominican friends were vegetarian, though. Maybe that was better, because as I started to eat my beans, I noticed that some of the pieces of pepper in it had legs. They weren't pepper at all, but some type of bug. I was so shocked, I couldn't even throw up. I looked around the table. Everyone was eating their beans so fast, they didn't even notice. I didn't want to alarm anyone, so I quietly requested that the group leader ask for the big bowl of beans in the middle of the table to be replaced with fresh beans. The restaurant owner obliged. I think that if I had told everyone, someone would have vomited on the table, maybe someone else would have screamed, and there would have been a big scene. What would you have done?

The next morning, we returned to Haiti to meet with workers who made clothing in a factory in Curacao. They had to sneak to meet us, because they could get fired or even killed for telling Americans about what was happening in the factories. I can't name the companies that they were making clothing for in this book because of legal reasons, but I promise you, you have shopped at *all* of them before. They are very big, famous, multibillion dollar corporations. So, you can imagine my surprise to find out that the workers were taking home less than a dollar per day, after working 8 – 12 hours. Most of them could only afford to eat once per day and it was difficult for them to pay to send their children to school. Some of them were physically attacked at work and many of the women were sexually harassed regularly.

The managers, which often were hired from other countries and not from Haiti, offered the women extra pay if they would have sex with them. Can you imagine? If you were working there, you may say, okay, I will do it because I want to feed my children three meals today. It is such a horrible situation. Fortunately, there are steps that you can take to stop these types of travesties from continuing to happen. Let's take a break and cover five of them!

--

5 Things that You Can Do This Month to Promote Human Rights in the Garment Industry:

1.  Sign petitions related to Human Rights on avaaz.org, change.org, or another social justice petition site. Petitions really do help.

2.  Show a documentary such as *Life and Debt* or *Mickey Mouse in Haiti* to your friends, family, school, club, or religious organization to raise awareness. Visit http://filmsforaction.org to find lots of free streaming documentaries.

3.  Become a more conscious consumer by researching companies before purchasing

clothing from them.  You can also visit
http://www.sweatfree.org/shoppingguide to
see a list of sweat free companies.

4.  Organize a campaign at your high school, at
    your college, or in your community to promote
    purchasing clothing from companies that pay
    a living wage.  A living wage, according to MIT,
    is "the approximate income needed to meet a
    family's basic needs[***]".

5.  Hold clothing swaps with your friends keep
    cool fashion circulating while cutting down the
    amount of sweatshop produced clothing being
    purchased.

--

I returned to Haiti for the second time in May
2014, to collect interviews about the 2010
earthquake and to set up medical clinics for people in

---

[***] http://livingwage.mit.edu/

tent cities. Tent cities are exactly what they sound like, cities made of tents. Families of five usually live in tents smaller than your living room.

Can you imagine sharing such a small space with your whole family *and* everything that you own? As you can picture, many times people are literally sleeping on top of their stuff. This is probably a good thing, because there are no locks on tents. There is no way to prevent a robber or worse from entering. It's a hard life. What makes it especially hard is that most of these areas also do not have access to clean water or fresh fruits and vegetables. Picture 100,000 tents crowded together on a small patch of dry land surrounded by broken concrete where the earthquake has demolished homes and buildings. That is a tent city.

We brought lots of medicine with us to treat various illnesses. After a short time, I started to notice patterns in the patients. Many of them had the same types of parasites and infections. I asked the medical doctor who we brought with us why this was the case. He showed me research once we arrived back at the guest house where we slept. Most of the sickness was coming from simple lack of clean water, lack of fresh food, and lack of systematic preventative health. I was both heartbroken and empowered. I was saddened by so many people suffering over things that we take for granted in America, but empowered by knowing that these were problems that I could help solve.

I know that all of this sounds sad, but Haitian people are so strong, so welcoming, and so beautiful in spite of everything that has happened to them. I would like to share with you some of the poems that I was inspired to write by their beauty.

--

## The Art
I want to learn the art
Of carrying a load of plantains on my crown
Or scaling a barbed wire fence

Without tearing my clothes
Of proferring my children
Clean water to bathe
At 6:00 am, before the sun gets too hot;

I want to learn the art
Of creating beauty
Where others see
Nothingness
Of painting pineapples and papayas
Where others see
Poverty
Of my worship being stronger than my pain;

I want to learn the art
Of sewing fans from palm leaves
To cool my head
Of praying to God
When others would forsake
Of paying homage to my ancestors

Tomorrow Will Be Better 68

When others would forget

Because freedom is
Spiritual perseverance
Amidst struggle
Because freedom is always believing
That tomorrow will be better

Because freedom is hoping
When the world says there is no hope
And loving when you have every right to hate;
Freedom is living when death would be
understood.

--

## Parts for Sale

On a dusty street in Port au Prince
Stacked on red soil
Labeled in bright pastels:
A child's smile
With no language and no borders,

A grandmother's love
Always ready to give more,
A husband's strength
He will die to protect you,
A woman's devotion
To her family and her God,
A leader's guidance
When faith seems out of reach,
A teacher's patience
Through knowledge, empowered,
A pastor's courage
To provide for those who still believe,
A priest's magic, to curb off ill omens,
An artist's vision
To see a new world;
Parts for Sale
To create a New Haiti
With the people's needs at the center
And God's love at the head;
Parts for Sale.

# Containers

Bricks

To build your house

Tubs

To carry water

Jugs

For gasoline

Bowls

To carry yams

Bottles

For Coca Cola

Bags

For pure water

Sacks

For clean rice

Bins

For papaya and plantains

Tap Taps

For Human Cargo

And Bodies

Millions of Brown Bodies

For strong and bright souls

That daily

Struggle

Rise

Persevere

Renew.

--

My third voyage to Haiti was to plant fruit trees in areas where all of the trees had been chopped down, Anse-a-Pitre. On this trip, my son began traveling with me. As I am writing this, he is 10 years old. Doing service work internationally is so helpful and so rewarding, but fun too. We slept outside under mosquito nets on straw mats. Mountains stretched above our heads to a pitch black sky filled with millions of stars. I could only see a small fraction of these stars living in Houston, a heavily lit city. We were within walking distance of two beautiful beaches. One was covered in large smooth gray rocks. The other was covered in glistening white sand.

Volunteering was fun because we got to meet new friends from around the world and try new things, like cutting weeds with machetes. Also, when our volunteer shifts ended, we might just lay out on hammocks playing guitar and singing songs, use solar panels to watch a cool movie on a projector screen, walk into town to listen to live drumming or watch dance performances, or chill in the shade and relax. It was cold at night in Anse-a-Pitre, so one night, we walked 2 miles through the darkness to find a lady who sold freshly made hot chocolate. She cooked the bars of chocolate down in a big pot and mixed it with coconut milk and special spices. It was the richest, creamiest, and most delicious hot chocolate that I ever drank in my life.

My son went snorkeling for the first time off the coast of Anse-a-Pitre, Haiti. The ocean is yours – it's not filled with motorboats and tourists like the beaches in the United States. We held hands and swam out as far as he felt comfortable, then turned and swam back to shore. The beaches are so empty in the rural areas that you can even swim in your underwear. You don't have to worry about being stylish, in shape, or anyone judging you. You can just be free and enjoy life, while really making a difference.

## Chapter 5: Work Hard, Have Fun, Make a Difference

I mentioned to you that I traveled to Dominican Republic to interview garment workers in 2013. This is where I learned the most important lesson about service work that I will ever learn. You don't have to be boring to make a difference. It's important to have fun with it. Before I went to the DR with *Solidarity Ignite*, I thought that when you are helping people in another country, you should be all super serious, perpetually sad, and maybe even a little stressed. People are suffering, so why should I smile, right?

The first thing that we did once we arrived in the DR that year is go to the beach. Once we got there, we met other student organizers and workers from the factories. We ate delicious food on the sand and then swam together. What a great way to begin getting to know each other. Now, I'm sure we could have met in some drab office and told each other sad stories, but what would that accomplish? The best way to get to know someone is to really hang out with them.

The workers that we met that day were mostly women who worked at a small factory in a town called *Alta Gracia*. The factory is also called Alta Gracia. Let me tell you what our approach accomplished. I didn't just "meet" the workers from Alta Gracia, such as Yenny and Maritza. We laughed together, cried together, and danced together. I slept at their houses and met their children. They have a lifelong place in my heart. When you go volunteer, take time to have fun and really get to know the people. It will not only give you more passion for the cause, but you will have friends globally for life.

Alta Gracia is the *only* clothing factory in the entire country that pays the employees a living wage. In other words, the workers make enough money to pay for their food, clothing, and shelter. Also, they can take good care of their health, send their children to school, buy houses for their families, and still have a few dollars left to save for a rainy day. Because Alta Gracia is a small factory, students' efforts promoting it in the United States make a huge difference. Increased sales allow the company to hire more workers, which takes more people out of poverty. Correspondingly, improved sales provide greater job security for the current employees.

While Alta Gracia's employees were doing really well, there were also many workers struggling because they still worked in sweatshops. A sweatshop is a factory that pays very little, works the employees very hard, and usually has poor safety conditions. We spent time with workers who answered sales and service calls for major American telecommunications companies which I can't name. Our new friends had extremely crazy experiences at work. For example, at some companies, our friends could not go to the bathroom unless the preset schedule indicated that it was their time to go to the bathroom. This stringent rule even applied to pregnant women. What's worse, there were armed security guards standing in front of the bathroom doors to prevent our friends from breaking this outlandish rule. Another crazy thing -- it got super-duper hot inside of these call centers, because there was no air conditioning. Yet, instead of taking action to change the temperature, the managers would tell the workers to take their shirts off.

The injustices that were reported to us in Dominican Republic exist globally. The workers often form *unions*, or organized groups which identify collective demands and put pressure on their employers to meet those demands. Usually, these entreaties center on higher pay, better safety conditions, and fair treatment. At many times, their efforts result in some level of progress. However, they are more likely to be successful and at a greater speed if international advocates like you are involved. Reason being, the companies' main objective is to make more money and we, the Americans, control how much money that they make.

Americans are in most cases the *consumers*, or the people buying the products that the workers are generating. From a business perspective, if your employees complain, it doesn't mean as much as if your consumers complain. The employees do not have a lot of other options for work, so they cannot just quit and find another job. The unemployment rates are usually so high in developing nations that the citizens' most reliable source of income is to work for a factory that may cheat them, devalue them, or abuse them.

That is why your voice and your actions are important. Of course, there are challenging questions to come into play. For instance, many students ask me, "If we put too much pressure on the sweatshops, won't they just move their business to another country? Isn't it better to have a bad job than no job at all?" These are great questions. Let's apply this logic from a different perspective. If your one of your girl friends told you that her boyfriend was beating her ass every night, but paid her bills sometimes and bought her a car, would you tell her to stay or to leave? You would probably tell her to leave and have faith that she would find a better situation and a better man, right?

By the same reasoning, even if the factories do move to another country, the people are smart enough and creative enough to find other ways to survive. Eventually, the brands that support those factories will be forced to change their ways. They cannot just move their business to other countries forever. No matter where they go - Vietnam, Bangladesh, Honduras – we, the consumers, will continue to demand justice on behalf of the workers. Also, the workers will continue to form unions, organize strikes, and petition to be paid and treated fairly.

And remember, you can have lots of fun along the way! You can travel often and meet the workers yourself, you can show documentaries (with delicious snacks!) in your hometown, or you can think of other cool creative ways to engage the issues. Making a difference never has to be a drag. Yes, it is sad that bad things are happening to good people. But, it is okay to feel happy and powerful because you *can* change things for the better. Also, now that you know what is going on, you can teach your friends and get them involved too. You can be more than a hero – you can be a hero who makes heroes.

--

## 10 Steps to Take This Year to Make a Huge Difference

10. Start learning a new language. The more languages that you speak, the more people that you can communicate with effectively.

9. Write a letter to a government official about a local or international issue that you want to see change.

8. Join a social justice or human rights organization. Fellowship helps to keep us focused on our goals, while we make awesome friends!

7. Read a non-fiction book that will teach you more about global current events, such as *Half the Sky: Turning Oppression into Opportunity for Women Worldwide* by Nicholas Kristof and Sheryl Wudunn. Share what you learn with your friends.

6. Start making a written plan to volunteer abroad in a developing nation. Seeing the world helps us to understand it better.

5. Watch one documentary each week on filmsforaction.org. Watching films takes less effort than reading, but can be just as rewarding. The more you know, the more that you can help.

4. If there is no youth organization in your area that addresses local or global justice, pick an issue and start one at your high school, at your college, or in your community.  Here are some issues to think about as you choose your group's focus:  *Child Labor, Death Penalty, Economic Justice, Food and Hunger Issues, War, US Poverty, Globalization, Health Care, Water, Discrimination, Environment,* and *Human Trafficking* (pick one or more)[†††].  Within your organization, commit to learning more about your issue of choice and running at least two action based campaigns per year (i.e. protesting, letter writing, resource gathering and redistribution, rallying, etc...).

3. Use what you learn creatively.  Take something that you have learned from this book, from other reading, or from a film, and

---

[†††] List inspired by Education for Justice's Social Justice Resource Map.

create something!  You can write a poem, write a story, shoot a short film, compose a song, draw a picture, paint a painting, or whatever your heart leads you to do.  Share your creative work with others or sell it for a good cause.

2. Become knowledgeable about the world.  Each month, research a different country's history and current news to gain a more holistic view of humanity.

1. Start reading the news each morning.  News isn't just for old people.  Huffington Post, The Guardian, The Grio, and The Root are great sites to begin reading.

# Chapter 6: Go Back to Africa - Waking Up in Ghana

My very first international journey was to Ghana, West Africa to study Africana Oratory and Philosophy with students from the University of Houston African American Studies Department. We also distributed school supplies to children in need. Ghana is a choice country to visit for African Americans seeking to reconnect with Africa because of its beauty, safety, history, and culture. In Ghana, you can visit lush rainforests, gorgeous mountains, white sand beaches, lively street markets, palaces, museums, restaurants, and so much more! Ghana has it going on. The people were amazingly nice, the food was delicious, and the scenery was beyond beautiful.

While Ghana's magnificence is stunning, being there also awakened me to the difficult parts of our history. In the crowded town of El Mina, I crossed a bridge into what appeared to be a castle. All around the castle were bustling streets that smelled of fish and auto exhaust. We were very near the ocean. With each step that I took, my heart sank a little more. I could sense that I was entering a dark place. Underneath a towering castle like those from horror movies, lay the dungeons where African people were held before being shipped to America.

These dungeons had been built by European invaders, but also by groups of Ghanaians who assisted them. This was the hardest part for me to swallow. The Ashanti people of Ghana built their wealth and power through corroborating with the Europeans in enslaving their own people.

I hate to think that Black people would do this to other Black people. At the same time, I understand that the type of slavery that existed in America, chattel slavery, had not existed in Africa. Slavery in Africa had been more like a barter -- an exchange of service for food, clothing, and shelter. If you were enslaved in African civilizations, it did not mean that your children were also slaves, that your master could abuse your body, or that you were less than human.

Still, slavery is not right under any circumstance. Seeing that Africans participated in the slave trade made me want to forgive White people. I couldn't hold on to the anger that I had started to develop towards Europeans, because what they did to us, we also did to ourselves. There is good in the world and anyone is capable of being good. Likewise, there is evil and anyone is capable of practicing evil.

Every history has contradictions. Similarly, you will witness modern contradictions if you visit any African country. While many Black women in America are "going natural", many women in Africa wear perms and weaves. Also, even in the poorest towns, you will see people with cell phones. Even without electricity, people have cell phones. They may use a solar panel, a generator, or a car battery to charge them. Some people may view these contradictions as indications of African people not having their stuff together. I don't perceive it that way.

As far as Blacks enslaving Blacks, I look it at like the crack cocaine era here in the United States. Back in the 1980's and early 1990's, thousands upon thousands of Black Americans began either smoking crack or selling it. I don't think that anyone realized that it would destroy their bodies and destroy their families the way that it did. Likewise, I think that those who chose to sell crack were looking to build a type of wealth that they had only seen White Americans acquire. Many people built their first houses with crack money or started businesses that still survive today. During a time when it was difficult for Blacks to secure employment or loans, crack offered a relatively quick way to get rich.

When I was growing up, my grandmother and two of my uncles ran a lucrative business based on crack and marijuana. It helped my grandmother to feed us, to expand her legal businesses, and to purchase material items like guns, gold, and diamonds, that she hoped to leave as an inheritance for us. However, the crack game, like slavery, is violent and unpredictable.

Even with the best of intentions that the Ashanti might have had about spreading their empire to create a lasting legacy, they took part in actions that destroyed millions of lives. Similarly, in my family, there were horrendous repercussions. My grandmother had three sons. One of them got hooked on crack and stayed on it until his addiction killed him. The other two were imprisoned for long stints during her lifetime. All of her belongings that she hoped to leave behind were either stolen by the greedy, burned by the jealous, or sold by us to pay for her funeral. The only thing that she was able to leave for us was her sweet and strong spirit, which inspired me and taught me so much.

I say all of this not to spread my family's personal business or to speak ill of my grandmother.

She was a powerhouse of a woman who ran many successful legal businesses. What I want you to understand is that she didn't know crack would mess up her life and her son's lives, just like African people who helped sell other Blacks probably didn't understand what would happen to us once we arrived in the Caribbean and in the United States.

They didn't know that we would be tortured, raped, and treated like animals. Those were not normal practices in slavery historically. If they had known what was going to happen, they probably would have made different decisions. But now, we are free, strong, and intelligent. We can reconcile with our brothers and sisters in Africa and help each other to attain wealth and power legally.

Ghana is a great location for reconciliation to happen, because the government grants free land and dual citizenship to African Americans. This means that you can be a US citizen and a Ghanaian citizen at the same time. The free land is leased for 99 year contracts to promote Black Americans building homes and businesses in Ghana. While a three bedroom home may cost upwards of $100,000 in the United States, one can build the same size home for around $7,000 in Ghana currently. The prices rise each year, but not drastically. Also, one does not pay property taxes in Ghana. Once you build your home, you are not paying a monthly fee to anyone relating to it.

There is great potential for profitable businesses to be started in Ghana by African Americans. When I visited in 2011, we met with one of the president's representatives and he shared with us that we could start businesses in tourism, processing factories, or exporting with high opportunity for success. Ghana is a gorgeous country that attracts tourists from all over the world who would love to be guided by someone who speaks English fluently and can help provide them with American comforts such as soft beds and hot showers. People want to experience another country, but they also want to feel like they're still at home in a way. This is something to think about if you are business minded and open to travel.

Outside of the sadness of the slave dungeons, there was so much beauty in Ghana that I could have been in the Bahamas, or one of the other vacation spots that you see on television. We hiked through the rainforest and saw every kind of fruit tree that you can imagine. Do you like hot chocolate or coffee best? On our hike, we saw cacao trees, which is where chocolate comes from, and we saw coffee bean trees too! Have you ever seen a monkey up close and personal? As I was walking, a monkey climbed down on my shoulder to eat a banana that I had in my hand! Would you have been scared?

Ghana has the most peaceful and serene beaches that I have ever seen. Strong, muscular Ghanaian men stretched hammocks between coconut trees for us to lie on while we were at the beach, and lovely women dressed in bright colors cooked us local delicacies. Ghanaians eat a lot of fish. Not the fish that you see at the fast food joints either – these were *big* fish, twelve or fourteen inches long, cleaned and cooked whole over an open fire. The fish is served with fresh vegetables like cabbage and carrots, plantains, savory pinto beans, fluffy white rice, and always – with a soda. Ghanaians love soda. The crazy thing is that the Ghanaian soda does not have high fructose corn syrup and artificial colors in it like the soda does here. It is healthier and tastier.

While in Ghana, we learned how to crush recycled glass and melt it to create handmade jewelry. We also learned how to make these intricate artistic cloths with dye and wax called batiks and we learned to weave colorful African scarves called Kente cloth. You know, the ones like you see the African kings wearing on television. Speaking of kings, we visited palaces that were still filled with gold, detailed wooden sculptures, and valuable ancient artifacts.

There are still kings and queens in Ghana too. Not just one king and queen, but many; royalty in each region. I met one of the kings while there – he was very handsome and debonair. There was a queen there too – the queen of the Ashanti people in Kumasi. She was 106 years old and still pretty healthy.

Let me tell you a little about Ghana's history. Ghana was one of the great empires of ancient Africa. There were doctors, scientists, architects, artists, teachers, and agriculturists there, even thousands of years ago! The empire was bigger than the country is now. The modern day country of Ghana was colonized by the Portuguese in the 1400s and by the British in the 1800s. In 1956, Ghana gained its independence from colonization under President Kwame Nkrumah. He was a great man with tremendous visions for his country.

The story of Kwame Nkrumah teaches us an important lesson about why so many countries are suffering economically and politically now. At some point in your life, if you haven't already, you may ask yourself, "If Black people are so smart and Africa is so full of natural resources like gold and diamonds, why do we see all these starving kids and diseases on TV? Why don't they have electricity? Why aren't Africans balling?" You don't have to go study every African country to answer these questions. Instead, you can just study Ghana, the Democratic Republic of the Congo, and Kenya, and apply their histories to most countries that have been colonized. I will tell you about Ghana and you can study the other two countries on your own.

Kwame Nkrumah, the first president of Ghana, was an educated and charismatic man. He attended university in the United States, traveled the world, and wrote many books during his lifetime. When Ghana was on the brink of independence, Nkrumah ran his campaign for first president of free Ghana on the premise that he would build a hydroelectric dam that could provide electricity for the whole country.

Everyone was really excited about this, because they would quickly become a "developed" nation like Britain, France, and the United States.

The initial plan was to dig a massive manmade lake, the largest lake by surface area in the entire world. Once the earth was ploughed, the Bauxite (a precious mineral) beneath would be sold to Britain. The big hole for the lake was dug successfully. Unfortunately, Britain hit a financial crisis before the dam could be erected. In an elaborate plot to obtain control over Ghana, the United States and the International Monetary Fund (IMF) offered financial assistance towards building the dam. However, there was a catch.

The IMF does not give grants – it grants loans. These loans are accompanied by a contract that usually has many stipulations that can affect a country's economic and political climate. One of the conditions of Ghana's loan to build the Volta Hydroelectric Dam was that the electricity had to be set at the certain price per kilowatt. Economically, this makes sense. If you want a country to pay you back, they need to make enough of a profit from what you are investing into to be able to do so. However, the price at which electricity was set was and is too high for the average Ghanaian to afford. Thus, although there is a hydroelectric dam in Ghana that could hypothetically provide electricity to the whole country for free, most people in Ghana do not have electricity.

What can we learn from this story? First of all, not to trust a gift from those who do not have your best interests in mind. Americans and Europeans were not allies of Ghana at that time – they wanted to overthrow the president and replace him with someone that they could control and that did not have any socialist leaning ideas. Anything that made him look bad was good for them. In fact, the US CIA sent an agent into Ghana after the IMF contact was signed to arrange a *coup d'état*, or overthrow, of President Kwame Nkrumah. It was successful and

Nkrumah was exiled to Guinea, another West African country. If he had not trusted those who had historically been opponents of Ghanaian advancement, maybe the outcome would have been different.

Secondly, we learn from this story that it may be better to define our own idea of "development". Nkrumah believed that electricity was a symbol of development and was willing to go to great lengths to attain it. His other actions in Ghana, spending millions of dollars on modern architecture and monuments, also reflect investing a large amount of resources into playing catch up with European countries and the United States. In a way this was smart, because Ghana's architecture still attracts many tourists to bring money to the country. On the other hand, taking loans caused many people within the country to still not experience life anything close to how American tourists experience it while visiting.

Maybe, if Nkrumah had waited on electricity and put more money into making the country self-sufficient in the fields of business, agriculture, health, and education, maybe Ghana would be a stronger country today. But this is me looking at things in hindsight. Nkrumah being in that position during that time entailed pressures that I will probably never understand. For instance, would the people have still supported him if he backed out of building the dam when Britain reneged on buying the Bauxite? You remember being a kid and being really excited about going to some amusement park or Chuckie Cheese and then maybe your parents backed out at the last minute? It didn't matter what the reason was, you were going to bawl, right? By the same token, our leaders are not solely responsible when decisions are made that affect us negatively long term. At times, we the citizens encourage poor choices because we are also not thinking long term.

--

Tomorrow Will Be Better 99

# Assignment!

Find the movie "Lumumba" online and watch it. Write a two page journal entry about what you learned from the movie.

Consider these questions:

a. When Lumumba decided to change his speech, how did the Belgians respond?

b. Considering how quickly that everything happened, do you think that Lumumba could have done anything differently? If so, what could he have done?

c. Observe how the Belgians used both Lumumba's enemies and his friends against him. Why do you think that they chose this approach?

d. Mobutu the traitor was the president of the Democratic Republic of the Congo

(DRC) from 1965 to 1997. How many presidents has the DRC had since then? In comparison, how many presidents has the United States had from 1965 to today? What implications might the number of presidents have on the potential for change in a country?

# Chapter 7: Learn a Language: France and Spain

Do you speak any languages besides English? Speaking a second language is a valuable skill, just like learning to fix computers, wire a house, or plant a garden. When you have skills, you can go anywhere in the world and make money to survive. For example, if you learn to speak Spanish fluently, you can travel with a company or with a non-profit organization as a translator in a Spanish speaking country. Languages can be a source of income and travel opportunities.

I speak Spanish, French, and Haitian Kreyol currently on a conversational level. Spanish, I learned while waiting tables at a breakfast restaurant in Houston, Texas. We had many Mexican employees and customers whose English was limited. With French, I taught myself most of the first year with textbooks from a used bookstore and free online programs like *Duolingo*. By taking this approach, I was able to test out of some of the coursework and save money. I took my second year of French in an intensive course in France. Now that I am doing service work in Haiti, I am taking classes weekly to learn Haitian Kreyol, which is very similar to French.

I decided to take French as my official foreign language for my undergraduate degree because I already felt confident in basic Spanish and wanted to learn a language that would empower me to communicate with more people in the African Diaspora. Real talk, if you can speak English, Spanish, and French, you can communicate with most Black people around the world. Please remember that I said that and make an effort to become fluent in all three languages. So yes, I wanted to study French. And to gain an immersion in the language and culture, I wanted to study it in France.

Traveling to study abroad is easy, it just takes planning. First, I talked with the director of the French department at the university I attended

(University of Houston) about whether they had an opportunity to study in France. They did. If they had said no, I could have gone through a program outside of the university, like one the many programs listed on goabroad.com and studyabroad.com. Both of these websites also list scholarships to help you with your trip.

The keys to successfully getting funding to study abroad is having a decent GPA - 2.5 at the lowest, but aim for a *minimum* of a 3.0 – having a good essay, and meeting the required deadlines. If you have a good GPA, can write a decent essay, and are organized enough to meet deadlines, you can pull scholarships like pro ball players pull groupies, for travel, for tuition, and to have something left over just for you.

When I planned my trip to France, I applied for the Gilman International Scholarship for $3500, the International Educational Fee Scholarship for $1500, and a University of Houston undergraduate grant for $1000.  Between these sources of funding, and a little extra raised on an online crowdfunding site, I was able to cover a nearly $7,000 trip to study in Angers, France for 5 weeks at the *Université Catholique de l'Ouest*.  I lived with a French family there, who did not speak English.  While there, I attended school for usually 6 hours a day.

Angers (pronounced "Ahn-Jay") is a town about 90 minutes from Paris by train.  It is a lot like Paris really, as far as the local architecture, museums, nightly music scene, and wide array of museums.  At the same time, it is very different from Paris.  It is quieter, calmer, cleaner, cheaper, has less crime, and it has much more nature present such as forests and lakes.

My routine when I lived in Angers was to get up around 8:00 am, catch the public bus to school to arrive at 9:00 am, go to my classes (which were all fun), take a 90 minute lunch around noon, go to my next classes, and get out of school around 4:00 pm or

5:00 pm. After school, I would walk around town and explore, shop, check out museums, listen to live music, go swimming at the Sports Center, eat local foods, or just chill. Around 8:00 pm, I had dinner with my host family. After that, I would study, read, Skype with my family and friends back home, and go to bed.

On the weekends, our whole student group from Houston would go on field trips to other areas around France. We visited lots of castles where super rich kings and queens used to live. That was cool, but my favorite part of the trip was going to the summer music festivals. I went to two while I was there. One was on World Refugee Day. A refugee is someone who leaves his or her country because some crazy political stuff or violence is happening there and seeks safety in another country.

I met a number of amazing people from various African countries in Angers on World Refugee Day. We ate together – food from various East

African and North African countries.  Someone brought free paint and canvasses and we painted together.  Then, there was a big free concert with African drumming and Hip-Hop music.  It was unlike anything that I had ever experienced.

Then, a few days before I left Angers, there was a huge international music festival, simply called, *Fête de la Musique Angers*.  This means The Angers' Music Festival.  For over a 5 mile stretch, cars and buses were blocked from the streets.  Every block or so, a different band of a different genre was set up with a full stage and speakers.  This block, Salsa, the next block, Hip Hop, the next, Reggae, the next, Jazz, and so on.

I got there around 10:00 pm and started walking.  I was so overwhelmed by the sheer amount of people and music that I only spent a few minutes in each audience, trying to take in as much as possible in one night.  I walked and walked, seeing over 30 bands before 2:00 am. If you love music, this is the greatest high that you can ever experience.

When I finished my studies in Angers, I traveled back to Paris for a few days to enjoy all of the famous sights such as the Eiffel Tower, the Arc de Triomphe, and the Louvre museum. I slept in a hostel, which is like a dorm, but with people from all over the world.

What was Paris like? Amazing. The hostel was near a beautiful canal, a vast green park with caves and waterfalls, and the train station. I could just sit and watch the boats passing or walk through the park for free, or hop on the train to visit other parts of the city.

The night that I arrived in Paris, there was an open mic at the restaurant below the hostel. After listening to several truly phenomenal singers, I performed a love poem that received a great crowd response. This was one of my favorite moments in life. The energy, the smells of fresh baked bread and savory spices, making new friends from all over the globe, seeing the canal flowing through the wide glass windows, and sharing my creativity all at once!

Another great feeling about being in Paris was always meeting new people, from Senegal, India, Croatia, Canada – everywhere! I would meet a person and we would just immediately become friends. In many instances, I would have beautiful 2 or 3 hour conversations with someone that I just met. We might have dinner together or take a walk together at that moment and many invited me to come back and visit them in their home countries.

After a little time in Paris, I flew to Barcelona, Spain for four days. There, I also stayed in a hostel. In Barcelona, I tasted the best chocolate ever. There were these chocolate nougat covered almonds with a hard chocolate shell, dusted in chocolate. It was like three different flavors melting in my mouth at the same time! If you love chocolate like I do, you have to try these one day.  Next time that you go to a specialty store or Whole Foods here in the States, ask for cocoa dusted chocolate almonds from Barcelona.  You won't regret it.

Barcelona, like Paris, was full of music, paintings, sculptures, unique historical architecture, and super interesting people.  What is different about the two cities is that Barcelona is cheaper, warmer, has more trees and hiking paths, is mountainous, and has white sand beaches.  So, Barcelona wins.

In Paris, they speak French of course, but in Barcelona, they speak Catalan.  Catalan is like a mixture of Spanish and Italian and is spoken only in Barcelona.  I was able to get by speaking Spanish and English, and learned a little Catalan while there.  As long as you know how to read a map and say key phrases like "please", "thank you", "how much is it", and "where is the bathroom", you will be pretty much okay in most tourist locations.

My favorite moments in Barcelona were relaxing on the beach, enjoying art at the national museum, and riding the cable car up *Mont Juic*, a gorgeous mountain covered in a verdant forest. The national museum, Museo National de Catalunya (MNAC), is crazy magnificent. Each hall within it holds paintings and sculptures from a different era. Then, when you look up, even the ceilings are painted, similar to the Sistine Chapel. The outside of MNAC is just as lavish. It sits stop a mountain. The mountain is literally paved with four levels of rock stairs that lead down from the museum. Each level features a gushing hand designed waterfall lined with marble and colorful tiles and surrounded by flourishing gardens. Words cannot do it justice.

In Barcelona, my ankles were still terribly sore from my late night traipsing around the music festival back in Angers in cute little tennis shoes not appropriate for walking long distances. I was not in a position to hike up the mountains. So, I rode in cable cars; you know, like the skiers ride on television.

From the cable car going up Mont Juic, I could see all of Barcelona – the towering ancient buildings, houses every color of the rainbow, stretching fields of green, and the immeasurable blue ocean. At the top, there was a chapel, hundreds of years old. It featured stained glass windows with carved details that must have taken decades to complete. Next to the chapel was a small amusement park with a Ferris wheel and many rides. It was all so beautiful, I could have cried right there.

While cabling up another mountain, I found a treasure that gave me a new favorite spectator sport – water polo. Have you ever seen a water polo game? It's like soccer, but in the water. The swimmers use their hands and heads to knock the ball into the goal net. It is the most intense sport that I have ever seen. Basketball and football are pretty intense, but add to that the muscle stress of being in the water. So of course, the players had muscles out of this world. That's one of the great things about traveling – it opens you up to so many new things, even new sports.

After leaving Barcelona, I flew back to Paris before returning to the United States. I have not spent extensive time in any other European countries, but I have had brief layovers in Amsterdam and in United Kingdom. Being in Europe showed me what a country can be like when its culture and architecture is preserved. Many of the ancient monuments, homes, art pieces, and artifacts in Africa have been destroyed, damaged, or stolen – especially in West Africa. Consequently, while we can *read* about Africa's historical glory, much of what we see now is modern. Of course, this was in many cases because of Europeans. I viewed a huge amount of art in Europe that had been stolen from Africa. Still, it was great to be able to see it. I encourage you to also travel to Europe and have your own experiences, because they will enrich your understanding of the world as a whole.

# Chapter 8: Think Globally, Act Locally

What do Dr. Martin Luther King Jr., Malcolm X, Maya Angelou and Muhammad Ali have in common? All of their names start with an M of course, and you heard about them all during Black History Month, but what else? They have all been to Ghana. What do James Brown, Zora Neale Hurston, Langston Hughes, and Ralph Ellison have in common?

All of these greats -- their creativity was fed by international travel. What has been proven to improve students' grades and matriculation rates, while reshaping their worldviews? Studying abroad. Travel has always been important to great writers, activists, musicians, artists, singers, scholars, and teachers – really, anyone in any field who has sought to be great at what they do. With an open mind, you really cannot leave your home country and return unaffected.

Seeing the world does not mean that you abandon home. I still live in Houston and love my 'hood, but I have a better understanding of it and of myself now that I have seen how people live around the world. In 2011, in Houston, I was living in a 2 bedroom row house, less than 600 square feet. Anyone in America would have called it a tiny house. Within my little house, I had everything that I needed. I mean, I had a state of the art kitchen, fashionable furnishings in every room, and a central air and heat system. Yet, I was dissatisfied with my house because I was comparing it to others' homes who had more money than me.

Then, I went to Ghana. My host mother in Ghana lived in a house smaller than my living room. Her bed was a thin cot against the wall, a little smaller than her body. We sat outside on folding chairs, because there was no room for sitting inside. As we drank malted sodas and laughed together, she asked me how my house looked. In that moment, I felt ashamed to answer. I knew that I had so much more than her and did not want her to feel that her house was inferior.

Traveling to rural areas in developing nations like Ghana made me realize that what I thought was poverty, was privilege. I always have enough food, I never wash my clothes by hand, I control the temperature of my home to be warmer or colder, I always have clothes and shoes, I can read any book that I want for free by visiting the library or going online, and I have the ability to work and make money without fear of extreme verbal or physical abuse by my supervisor. I have the ability to apply for scholarships or grants to travel and learn, I can hold fundraisers to help those in need internationally, and I never have to worry about simple things like not being able to afford a pencil keeping me from going to school.

There are many problems here in the United States too, but recognizing my power and privilege makes me feel more confident to address them. I have a right to homeschool my child and the education to do so, so I do that. I also educate other children in my community and teach workshops in public schools. I have more than enough food, so my son and I feed the homeless regularly. I perform Spoken Word to raise awareness around local and global issues. I participate in campaigns, petitions, and protests to raise wages and improve safety conditions for workers locally and globally.

It's all connected, you see. Dr. Martin Luther King Jr. said, "An injustice anywhere is a threat to justice everywhere". You don't have to choose between helping your community and helping the world. You can do both. Sometimes, it's even easier to conquer a major problem internationally than it is here. Think of yourself as a warrior, winning little battles and big battles concurrently.

Let's talk about one of my good friends, Randryia Houston. When I met her, she was a young single mother living below the poverty line in

Houston.  Although she was not rich, famous, or married – she finished her undergraduate and master's degree in Social Work at the University of Houston by her mid-20's and started an international nonprofit organization, The Pencil Project, which focuses on collecting pencils and other supplies here in the US and distributing them to global communities in need in countries such as Ghana and Nicaragua.  She has donated over 200,000 pencils internationally to date.  While she has been changing lives around the world, she serves as a counselor and tutor to youth in her hometown – Houston, Texas.  Recently, she also started a business helping others to start nonprofit organizations.  She is a hero who makes heroes.

You see - what I want to emphasize here is that you don't have to *have* a lot to do a lot.  You don't have to just read about history, you can make history.  You don't have to be Brad Pitt or Angelina Jolie to do it either – you can be just a regular kid from the 'hood.  You can even be a kid with a record like my good friend Lamar who got into some trouble when he was younger involving drugs and robbery, but achieved his undergraduate degree from the University of Houston and his master's degree from the University of Louisville before being recruited as the Dean of a prominent school in Cameroon, West Africa. After completing his tenure there, he taught in South Africa, and then taught in Australia. He plans to start his own school one day based on all of his educating experiences in his hometown -- Houston, Texas. He is a hero to many although as I write this, he is barely 30 years old.

What problems have you identified in your community? Is there trash on the streets? Could you organize a group to pick up trash once a month? Does it get cold in the winter? Could you collect jackets, gloves, or blankets for those in need? Is there a community center in your neighborhood? Could you volunteer there? If there is no community center, could you reach out to churches and the local government and ask them to start one? Many feel powerless because they see problems, but cannot easily think of solutions. Many want to help, but feel that there is no real way to make a difference. Here are some ideas to help you brainstorm. Could you pick one of these to initiate this month or come up with your own?

## Things We Can Do to Make Our Communities Better

- ✓ Be good to each other.
- ✓ Feed the homeless.
- ✓ Pick up trash.
- ✓ Volunteer with or start a community garden.
- ✓ Study, promote, and practice good nutrition, self-care, and fitness.
- ✓ Mentor.
- ✓ Take parenting classes if you plan to be a parent one day. Better parents make a better world.
- ✓ Take or teach self-defense classes. Strong people make strong communities.
- ✓ Attend financial literacy and/or entrepreneurial workshops. Healthy finances are a part of a healthy community.
- ✓ Tutor a struggling student.

- ✓ Study the history of your culture.  If we know where we came from, we will have a better sense of where we're going.
- ✓ Cook a meal for an elder once per week.
- ✓ Write a letter or send a book to someone in prison.
- ✓ Babysit for a single parent.
- ✓ Start or join your neighborhood watch.
- ✓ Smile, give hugs, and say "I love you".

--

Another part of thinking globally is understanding histories of other oppressed people and how they overcame or are overcoming oppression.  As an African American woman, I grew up feeling like Black people had it the worst.  Maybe my Mexican friends felt like Mexicans had it the worst.  As I learned about other cultures, I realized that people all over the world have been through extreme challenges.  As human beings, we have more in common than we have as differences.  I would like to share two poems with you to inspire thought about global challenges.

The first poem, I wrote while visiting a photographic exhibit at the Jewish Holocaust Museum in Houston.  After seeing photographs taken in survivors' homes, I sat in an auditorium surrounded by elderly Holocaust survivors.  When they were just children, they were living witnesses to the most tragic catastrophe of the past century.  Now they live on as reminders of how hatred can blind us to our humanity if we let it.  Many of them are the only living survivors of their birth families.

The photograph that stood out the most to me in the exhibit was that of an unorganized stamp collection.  The survivor who collected the stamps asked the photographer why she chose to feature his messy stamp collection as art.  His wife was embarrassed too, because she kept the house immaculate.  Yet, he had postponed organizing this room full of stamps for over 60 years.  The photographer explained, in response to their confusion, that she was interested in what people choose to collect and how it reflects their identity.  I

was so struck by the whole interaction that I wrote
this poem. Please enjoy.

--

### Stamp Collection

When he was 9, his father handed him the first

stamp,

A train,

A sign of the Industrial Era,

Of progression and possibility;


He placed it neatly into a special book

Where he began to organize many types of

trains,

Lindbergh's plane, and Ford's automobiles,

Symbols of flight

And movement;


The stamp collection stayed behind

With his mother's teapots and his father's knives

When the men grabbed them,
Father, Mother, Little Sister,
And brought them to a dark place that
smelled like men's clothes after deer hunting
Or the butcher's shop at the very end of the
day;

Everything went black now
When he tried to think back
To Auschwitz;
He could only recall longing
For his father
And his stamp collection.

Time passed,
A Transatlantic Journey,
A Korean War,
Struggle towards new beginnings,
Little triumphs,
Marriage,

Children and children of children;

Years passed
Where he did not *care*
About the word: survivor,
Instead,
He stared into his coffee until it grew cold,
Trying to recall his mother's smile,
That song his father sang,
The game he and Little Sister played in the yard
The day before it all bled into one blur
That made him wish
He had been older,
Or smarter,
Or martyred,
So that all of these pieces could make sense
again;

And he spread out his stamp collection,
Anne Frank, Dr. King, Kennedy,

Neil Armstrong, Gandhi, Mandela,
Mother Teresa, Princess Diana, Michael
Jackson,
So many generations, gains, losses,
Had come and gone,
While he lived on;

Sitting in stacks and stacks of thumbnail sized
memories,
Mementos of the past,
Reminders of history,
Crisscrossing in ethereal labyrinths
That his wife called an embarrassment;

His personal path from the past to the present
He allowed to amass into ranks, pillars, and
orbits
But *refused* to organize
Because if there was one thing that he had
learned,

*Life* was not organized neatly.

--

This next poem is about a group not often mentioned in the history books, the Dalits of India. Because of their dark skin, they have been designated to the lowest caste of their country. Many live like slaves, even today. The only jobs that they can get in most cases are doing work that is considered dirty, like cleaning latrines (toilets) or butchering animals (which involves a lot of blood and waste). Many of the girls are forced into prostitution, to sexually serve men who have a lot of money and power.

Dalits who revolt are often persecuted, tortured, or killed. They are still fighting for their freedom today. I hope that this poem inspires you to learn more about them. We need social justice warriors now more than ever. As Fannie Lou Hamer stated, "Nobody's free until everybody's free".

--

## Untouchable

When her aunt returned her for the evening,
Rani pointed to the photo and said,
"Yellow.  Pink.  Green.  Blue!"
Babu smiled because 8 was not too old to
learn colors
When one was not supposed to learn at all.

He took Rani in his arms and served dal
From one brass pot
Rice from another,
He could not get flour for roti today,
Maybe he would sell the brass pots tomorrow,
And buy the thin kind shipped from America,
But would they burn on an open fire?

He thought about these things and smiled
As he watched Rani talking on and on
About a lizard she had seen today, and given
a name,

Poori, like the bread that rose fat as the fold of
the lizard's neck,
And Babu thought about the power to name
And how Rani may never have to know what a
"Servant of God" means here,
A servant by body to the upper caste,
If only he can find
More latrines to clean, or a second job,
Or somehow, get to America.

But that was just a dream, in a world
Where he was not clutching prayer beads
Nights when he heard footsteps
Moving too fast, or gunshots,
Tearing the air like fists in revolution
Because they might come for Rani
Like they did her mother, who did march,
And demand to be human, not
"untouchable",

Demanded rights from those who knew only
wrong
Who followed her home, before she could
fetch
Rani from Sita, before she could catch
Her breath, or set her body down, they pulled
her
Into the dusty street in an outrage,
Ripped the jeans, the ruffled blouse
From her body, "You try to be American!"
"You whore!" and they touched her, this
untouchable,
Intimately, violently, publicly,
Until she cried and bled and begged
For life.

Her body was burned
After being paraded down the path in
example
To others who thought about rights.

That was when Rani was only a baby,

He taught her now, from the 7 years of

schooling he had,

All that he knew.

And rebelled in a quiet way,

With education, with brass pots,

Which Dalits were not meant to own.

With the photograph of Buddha on the wall,

Which was forbidden,

And with his undying love for this girl child.

But most of all,

With the meat knife he kept near as they slept

In case smoke crept in through the open door

And he heard the sounds of chaos

Then he would recite the Buddhist prayer

"May all beings be free from suffering,"

And end hers quickly

Before they could make her body

An object.

# Chapter 9: Mansa Musa to Mike Brown: Why History Matters

Throughout our conversation, I have repeatedly mentioned history and historical figures. But why is history so important, anyway? That was then, and this is now, right? Well, not quite. History can inspire us presently to achieve greater goals. The richest man in history was a Black man from Mali, West Africa -- Mansa Musa. He was richer than Bill Gates, Oprah, and everyone who has lived since died over 700 years ago! He is the richest known human being of *all* time.‡‡‡ The next time that you hear someone say something about how White folks or Asian folks know how to get money, but Black folks can't ball like that, remember Mansa Musa.

Have you ever read about Maya Angelou? She was a great poet and author who spoke 7 languages

---

‡‡‡ http://www.independent.co.uk/news/world/world-history/meet-mansa-musa-i-of-mali--the-richest-human-being-in-all-history-8213453.html

and traveled all over the world. She was raped as a child and by her teen years, was a single mother who was forced to sell her body to support her child. During her lifetime, she assisted in the Civil Rights movement, performed at Bill Clinton's presidential inauguration, and received honors globally for her writing and activism. Maybe you have been through some rough situations too. When you feel like your circumstances determine your destiny, you can think about Maya Angelou and all that she accomplished.

Also, history can reveal solutions to problems that we face now. Over the past few years, two unarmed African American teens who were killed by law enforcement gained international attention – Trayvon Martin and Mike Brown. Have you ever read about Emmett Till, an unarmed teen killed for whistling at a White woman in the 1950s? Have you heard about Amadou Diallo, Oscar Grant, and Jordan Davis – unarmed youth who were all shot in the last decade? They were shot not because they had committed any crimes, but because the shooter hated or feared them based on their appearance.

If the same crimes happen over and over, then we cannot continue to just move on and say, "That's old news." There is an underlying problem that needs to be solved. We can study history to identify patterns and also to learn of solutions which have been applied in the past. That way, we can ascertain what worked well, what did not work well, and what remains to be tried.

Can you imagine a world where unarmed Black youth being shot is not a norm? Can you imagine a world without poverty, without starving children, and without people dying daily from preventable diseases? Can you imagine a world where everyone has everything that they need and people treat each other with respect and dignity? That is the kind of world that you can help create.

The thing is, we often read about history and feel separate from it. Booker T. Washington helped start over 5000 schools in the South during one of the most racist times in American history. Marcus Garvey started an economic movement that pooled millions of dollars from the African American community to start local and international businesses. When we read history, it's not just for learning -- it's for application.

If we each took a role in being *history makers*, then how many modern day Civil Rights and Human Rights leaders would we have? How many schools would we build? How many people in need would we serve? We have enough wealth and enough intelligence between all of us to solve every major problem in this world.

Marcus Garvey stated in the early 1900s, "The question often asked is what does it require to redeem a race and free country. If it takes man power, if it takes scientific intelligence, if it takes education of any kind, or if it takes blood, then the 400,000,000 Negroes of the world have it." This still stands true, not just for African Americans and Africans, but for people of any ethnicity. We have what it takes to make the world better.

Now, I would like to share two poems with you. This first poem was inspired by the "no indictment" decision by the grand jury for the murderer of Mike Brown, Darren Wilson. When I heard the decision, I cried. Then, I wrote this poem.

The title, Cut to Commercial, reflects the nonchalant attitude that much of the American population have begun to take towards the murder of Black youth. Many tried to justify Mike's death by stating that he was a thug, that he stole cigars, or that he may have intimidated the officer. Regardless of if he was a "thug" or not, the officer could have used a Taser or called for backup. The first line of response should not *ever* be ending someone's life. I hope that this poem inspires you to stay sensitive, to always stand for justice, and to never let real issues *cut to commercial*.

## Cut to Commercial

This is The Hunger Games,
A hunger untamed
To frame
Black bodies with chalk lines;

This is American Horror live,
Sorcerers in disguise,
Circle yourself with
Holy water and salt lines;

This is TV reality, listen,
*Chopped* and *Hell's Kitchen*,
Young black males on the chopping block
With scorched dreams and slayed visions;

This is *The Purge*,
Spraying bullets and words,

*How to Get Away with Murder,*

Tell them forget what you heard,

Forget what you saw,

Forget what you think,

And let the perpetrator back out on the streets

To keep peace;


Cut to commercial.


This is Emmett Till,

Revisited,

I saw this before;


This is Amadou,

Revisited,

I heard this before;


This is Trayvon,

The sequel to the sequel to the sequel,

This is a pilot light to ignite

The flame under the people,

This is a testament of evil,

This is not post racial,

This is America's selfie

In the age of no labels,

Post Raven Simone statement,

Everyone is an amalgamation

Until you have your day in court

Then it's like you just got off the slave ship;


Cut to commercial.


They say, they say,

"They say he stole a box of swishers."

"He was a big dude."

"He had weed in his system."

"I heard that he pushed him."

"This is not about race."

"You have to trust the system."

"He was in the wrong place."

Tomorrow Will Be Better 139

"It's blacks shooting blacks 'bout every damn
day."
"He probably wasn't doing nothing
With his life anyway."
Cut
To
Commercial.


Has human life become so worthless?
Have we abandoned our brothers?
Become without purpose?
We talk about who died to vote,
But who died so that we wouldn't go in circles?
It's time to stand in unity,
And not let this --
Cut
To
Commercial.

--

This next poem discusses the importance of remembering history, while also engaging an approach to conceptualizing solutions. We must remember all of the men, women, and children who sacrificed their time or their lives for us to have the freedoms that we do today. Ida B. Wells spent her life documenting the deaths of unarmed Black men about 100 years ago. If we are constantly forgetting our ancestors' sacrifices, what were their lives worth?

The title of this poem, "The 16th Strike", is based on a martial arts concept which states that there are only 15 techniques with which you can strike. The 16th Strike is when the spirit comes down and takes over. Many people feel that prayer and faith are important approaches to change, and they are. But in addition to that, we need to try solutions from every possible angle. Education, food, healthcare, political participation -- yes, yes, yes, yes! Whatever you can think of – yes, do that! Only after we have tried all of our best ideas, and all of our

worst ideas, can we say that we've done all that we
can.

--

### The 16<sup>th</sup> Strike

Bones Scattered

Over unmarked graves

Therein lie our ancestors

Bearing spears

Clutching cowry shells

And small children

In defiance

In dignity


Golden Arches for tombstones

Dungeons renamed castles

Chains of bondage

Renamed artifacts

History

Deemed irrelevant

Because we do not

Remember


Boom

We hear the world implode


Boom

We hear our souls explode

Like raisins in the sun

Because we do not

Remember


This

Is the 16th Strike

We must rise up from the pits of our souls

The pits in the soil

Where 500 Haitians lied buried alive up to their

necks

In biting insects

We must rise up from the pits of our souls


Tomorrow Will Be Better 143

Rise up like the swords and axes

Of Turner's men

Slicing

At the heads of oppression

Reclaiming dignity by force


We must rise up from the pits of our souls

Rise up from the gates of Hell

Like Satan – Malcolm

El Hajj Malik El Shabazz

Swooping down as Phoenix

A lightning bolt through the dull drumbeat

Of marching feet

To create a cadence

A new step

For all of history to dance to


By any means necessary

By any means necessary

We will regain human rights

By any means necessary

We will reclaim dignity


Microphone feedback

Gunshots

White hoods

Crosses aflame

Dinknesh

Sengbe

From the bones cradled in the belly of the land

of burnt faces

To the bones cradled in the belly of *La Amistad*

The "Friend" Ship

How long will we remain separate

From our native names?

Bones scattered

Unmarked graves


This

Is for the Zulu

The Mau Mau

For those who did not march

Who did not drink the Maji Maji

Who took up arms like Huey P.

Who jumped headfirst

From the Good Ship Jesus

Into the mouths of sharks

As sharks yelled from above

"Loss of profit!  Loss of profit!"

Loss of prophets…


Go down, Moses

Go down


This

Is for Araminta

Harriet Tubman

Fighting pigs

For food scraps

Following the North Star

As a road map

Reaching into empty pockets for destiny

Knowing there has *got*

To be something better


This

Is for Garvey

The flag still waves red

In the blood shed

Black

Green

Time

Has painted the Black Star Line

Red and Blue

Carnival Cruise Line


And will we sit by idly?

Will we sit by

Or remember?

Tomorrow Will Be Better 147

This is in their memory
This is for their dignity


Eighty pound Black bodies
Swooned
Under the crushing pressure of fire hoses
Teenage warriors
Flesh torn in the stinging clasp
Of teeth canine
This
Is for 4 Little Girls
Bodies spraying into the air in charred embers
Into the night air
This
Is for Carl Hampton
For every Black neck hung
For every Black body cut, torn, tarred,
feathered
Shot Down

This

Is for Oscar Grant, Ayanna Jones, Trayvon

Martin,

Jordan Davis, Mike Brown


This is for Imhotep, Narmer, Nefertari, Makeda

White images of Egypt mask our hidden history

This is for *Sankofa*

Reclaim the ancient mysteries

We must remember


This

Is the 16th Strike

250 years to life

Digging our own graves

With tired hands

Torn bodies

Amidst cotton fields

Sugar cane

Emancipated

To poll taxes

Sharecropping

Minimum wage

Aids warfare

Medication

14 plus years of education

To brown nose, eat dirt

And follow the program

Because we have to?


This

Is the 16th Strike

The aye covering our necks and faces

The ase, the ase, the ase-ooooooooooooooooo

The ancestors rise within us

Our bodies as altars

As a compass to dismember

We must remember

To do, all that we can

To do, all that we can

Tomorrow Will Be Better 150

And when we cannot

When we cannot

Then the spirit will come down like the yellow

fever

That took out the British troops in Ayiti

And rebuild our people

From freedom up

From freedom up

To dignity.

--


The poem that you just read also serves as a history primer for the African Diaspora.  Hop on Google and look up every person, place, or word that is foreign to you from that piece.  It will take you from ancient history to today – from Dinkesh to Trayvon, from Mansa Musa to Mike Brown.


--


List of People, Places, Events and Terms to Research:

- El Mina (Ghana)
- Malcolm X (El Hajj Malik El Shabazz)
- "The Land of Burnt Faces"
- Dinknesh
- La Amistad
- Zulu
- Mau Mau
- Maji Maji uprising of Tanganyika
- Good Ship Jesus
- African Holocaust
- Araminta (Harriet Tubman)
- Marcus Garvey
- Black Star Line
- Children's March (Civil Rights Era)
- 4 Little Girls
- Emmett Till
- Carl Hampton (shot)
- Oscar Grant (shot)
- Ayanna Jones (shot)
- Trayvon Martin (shot)

- Jordan Davis (shot)
- Mike Brown (shot)
- Imhotep
- Narmer
- Nefertari
- Makeda
- Sankofa
- Aye: a clay used for spiritual ceremonies
- Ase (pronounced ah-shay): power, spirit, energy
- Yellow Fever in Haitian Revolution

## Chapter 10: Get Engaged (and I ain't talkin' about putting a ring on it)

Now, it is time that take all that we have shared here and put it into action. Ask yourself these questions: What are you passionate about? What do you know? What can you teach? What languages do you speak fluently? Can you grow food to feed yourself? Can you fight to defend yourself? What do you have to offer? What are you mastering? How are you making yourself valuable in the world? What do you want to accomplish before death? What is your purpose for being? These are tough questions, and may take a few years to answer but they are worth taking the effort to answer.

Life is not about just getting a good job, a place, and a car. Life is not just about pleasure or having fun. All of these things are important to a peaceful and joyous life, but they are not an end goal. Think about who you look up to or admire. Write down the names of 5 people who inspire you here.

_____

_____

_____

_____

_____

Now, what are the main characteristics of these 5 people? Are they strong, charismatic, organized, intelligent, honest, wise, hardworking, etc...? Write down 10 adjectives that describe your inspirations here.

_____

_____

_____

_____

_____

_____

_____

_____

_____

_____

The next question to ask yourself is, do you also embody these characteristics? If not, you can cultivate them? Anything that another human has ever done, you are capable of doing.

What are some of the goals that you would like to achieve during your time on the planet? These can range from graduating from college to eliminating world hunger. Please write 10 down here, no matter how small or how ambitious.

_____

_____

_____

_____

_____

_____

_____

_____

_____

_____

Are there people in your life who are supportive of you in reaching your goals? They can be friends, family, mentors, teachers, or religious leaders. Please write as many as you can think of here. Use an extra sheet of paper if you need one.

_____

_____

_____

_____

_____

_____

_____

_____

_____

Now that you have it on paper what you would like to see for your life and who can help you along the way, you can set short term goals and long term goals to help you manifest the life you want. Short term goals can range from tomorrow to 6 months, while long term goals usually fall within the next 1 – 10 years.

Start keeping a journal and recording your short term and long term goals, along with daily thoughts. You can also write down motivational quotes that you hear or find online. This is a practice that has helped me tremendously over the past 5 years. As a result of journaling, goal setting, and putting in the required work, I have traveled to 9 countries, learned 3 languages besides English, won numerous scholarships, published books, produced my own Web Series, started my own business, and I am now helping people in other countries to meet their basic needs. I wouldn't recommend something to you that has not worked in my own life.

I started this book by telling you about my childhood and some rough situations that I have had to overcome. As I shared with you, I did not get my GED until I was 22 years old. As I write this, I am 29 years old and I have been featured on television, on numerous radio shows, and in newspapers because of what I have made of my life. I pray that my life can be a testament to you that where you start does not have to be where you finish. Maybe you have been through some challenges too. Maybe they were more serious than mine, or maybe not as serious. Either way, you can still do incredible things with your life.

My life is in a space now where knowing has overlapped doing and knowledge has met opportunity. I hope to write an incredible autobiography one day for you, expressing the fullness of beauty and service that my life has embodied. Trust me, I'm just getting started. I hope to continue to help many people as I grow. Meanwhile, I hope that you have gained from my journey so far and that it adds a little to your purpose. Thank you for reading. I love you.

# Stuff to Check Out

## Books:

*No Disrespect* by Sister Souljah

*The Hood Health Handbook Vol. 1 and 2,* edited by Dr. Supreme Understanding

*Lady's Man* by Dr. Obari Cartman

*Manchild in the Promised Land* by Claude Brown

*I Know Why the Caged Bird Sings* by Dr. Maya Angelou

*Black Boy* by Richard Wright

*The Bluest Eye* by Toni Morrison

*Lessons from History Advanced Edition* by Dr. Jawanza Kunjufu

*A Piece of Cake: Memoir* by Cupcake Brown

*Seed to Harvest Series* by Octavia Butler

*Gorilla, My Love* by Toni Cade Bambara

*For Colored Girls...* by Ntozake Shange

*Sacred Woman* by Queen Afua

*The Spirit of Intimacy* by Sobunfu Some

*Letters to a Young Sister* by Hill Harper

*Letters to a Young Brother* by Hill Harper

*How to Hustle and Win: A Survival Guide for the Ghetto* by Dr. Supreme Understanding

*Black Men: Single, Obsolete, and Dangerous?* by Haki Madhubuti

*Rich Dad, Poor Dad* by Robert Kiyosaki and Sharon Lechter

*48 Laws of Power* by Robert Greene and Joost Elffers

*Don't Sweat the Small Stuff* by Richard Carlson

*The 21 Indispensable Qualities of a Leader* by John Maxwell

## Websites:

Check out Randryia Houston's site, Unleash Your Movement: http://unleashyourmovement.com. Also, be sure keep in touch with me through http://nikalaasante.com.

## Videos:

Pharaoh the Web Series (Youtube)

16th Strike the Documentary (Vimeo)

# Acknowledgments

First and foremost, all praise be to God for bringing me this far and allowing me to have a purposeful position in the world. Thank you to those who have had great influence in my life, to those who have let me cry on their shoulders, and to those who have supported me through joys and challenges. Thank you to my mother and father for always doing your best. Thank you to my sisters – Stacie, Rachel, and Martina – for your love. Thank you to Grandma Dorothy and Aunt Lonnie Mae for your supportive spirits and consistent support.

Thank you to Deloyd Parker and to my SHAPE Community Center family. Thank you to Rick Lowe and my Project Row Houses family. Thank you to Dr. Malachi Crawford for your friendship and for the tremendous guidance that you have provided to me in growing as a writer, as a scholar, and as a human being. Thank you to Dr. Conyers and my African American Studies Program family. Dr. Conyers, my first voyage out of the country was thanks to your fundraising efforts. I can never thank you enough. Thank you to Baba Shango and my SEHAH family.

Thank you to Dr. Shasta Jones Theodore and Bienvenu Theodore for your guidance, love, and friendship. Thank you to Dr. Carl Lindahl for your support and mentorship. Thank you to Dr. Claudine Giacchetti for believing in me and being supportive. Without your efforts, I would never have studied in Europe. Thank you to Mama Mawiyah Buseje for walking this path first, thus making it easier.

Thank you to Randryia Houston and Lamar Johnson for your inspiration, friendship, and allowing me to tell your stories. Thank you to Rachel Taber and Amy Kessel for making it possible for me to become an international advocate of Human Rights. Thanks ladies, for opening my eyes to important realities and showing me how to have fun in the process.

Thank you to Toni Alika Hickman for providing spaces for me to perform and spotlighting my work in your important documentary, 16<sup>th</sup> Strike. I love you, sis.

Special acknowledgements to Kimberly Williams, Dr. Frank Anderson, Dr. Ayanna Abdallah, Dr. Perry Khepera Kyles, Michelle Barnes and Community Artists' Collective, Melissa Betts, Stephanie Betts, Kathy Smathers, Julie Tolliver, Perri McCary, Deirdre Danner, Amani Osun, Sally Harris, Neshama Alheem, Neeki Bey, Willie Jamaal Wright, Vivian McKelvey, Jon St. Mary, Derek Michael Parker, David Sha, Cyntha and Ali Muhammad, Troy and Happy Amazulu, Angelica B. Molina, Lavita Ru, and Velyjha Southern for your support. There is no me without you.

Special shout outs to Wali of All Real Radio, Akua Holt of the Pan African Journal, Christian Tucker of KCOH, Brother Jamaal of Inner Light Radio, Doc and J of Reggae Bodega, and Deepak Doshi of Doshi House for consistently supporting my work.

Meda ase to Kolade for helping me to stay centered. Thank you Tariq Houston for your love and insights. Thank you to Akingbe for always being that one I can call on and for listening to my poetry before anyone cared. Thank you to Jon Goode for always being first in line to support and show love. Thank you to Dylon Killian – Cola Rum – for helping shape who I am as a Spoken Word Artist. You pushed me to perform with all of my soul and killed my timidity. Thank you.

I would like to give a giant thank you to my son – my heart, my love, my motivation. One day you will read this and say, "Wow, my mom is pretty cool," and you'll be inspired to be even cooler.

If there is anyone is neglected to mention, charge it to my head and not my heart. I love you all and I am so thankful for you all. Truly.

Made in the USA
San Bernardino, CA
04 July 2015